COOK WITH KIDS

I'd like to dedicate this book to my beautiful family. Tabitha, Jasper and Imani and my lovely wife Amber, who can rattle a pan in her own right.

COOK WITH KIDS

ROB KIRBY

ABSOLUTE PRESS

First published in Great Britain
in 2011 by **Absolute Press**
Scarborough House
29 James Street West
Bath BA1 2BT
Phone 44 (0) 1225 316013
Fax 44 (0) 1225 445836
E-mail info@absolutepress.co.uk
Website www.absolutepress.co.uk

Reprinted 2011.

Publisher Jon Croft
Commissioning Editor Meg Avent
Art Direction Matt Inwood
Design Claire Siggery
Photographer Lara Holmes
Food Stylist Rob Kirby
Editor Joanna Wood

ISBN **9781906650582**

A catalogue record of this book is
available from the British Library.

Printed and bound in Slovenia.

A note about the text
This book was set using Sabon and
Univers. Sabon was designed by
Jan Tschichold in 1964. The roman
design is based on type by Claude
Garamond, whereas the italic design
is based on types by Robert
Granjon. Univers is a clear legible
sans-serif font designed to be used
in longer stretches of text. It was
created in 1954 by Adrian Frutiger
for the French type foundry,
Deberny & Peignot.

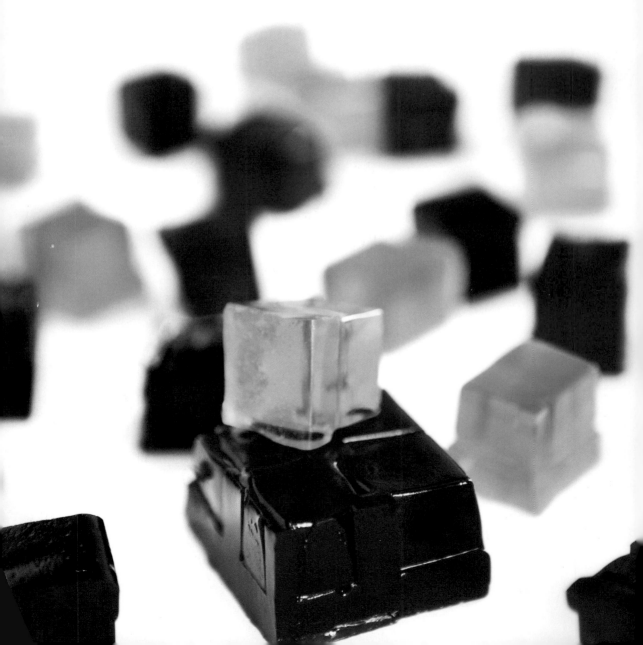

FOREWORD BY
HESTON BLUMENTHAL

COOKING IS ONE OF THOSE DECEPTIVELY
ORDINARY, EVERYDAY THINGS THAT CAN
PULL A FAMILY TOGETHER IN OUR
FRAGMENTED SOCIETY, BUT IT'S A RARE
COOKBOOK THAT CAN SUCCESSFULLY
COMBINE RECIPES THAT WILL APPEAL
TO BOTH KIDS AND THEIR PARENTS.

I've known Rob as a chef at the top of his game for several years
now and one of the best things about him is his instinctive
understanding that food infused with a good dollop of fun in its
making is the key to stimulating anybody's interest in cooking
and eating good food. That's particularly true of youngsters.

Cook with Kids is bright, breezy, sophisticated and full of great
recipes that will get you, your kids and the rest of the family in the
kitchen making food together. Better than computer games and
telly, any day!

HESTON BLUMENTHAL, BRAY, JULY 2011

INTRODUCTION

This book is about cooking with kids and it got me thinking not only about the Children's Hospital School at Great Ormond Street Hospital in London (without whom this book wouldn't exist), but also about my own childhood; and how food played such a huge part in that.

I grew up in the 1970s in north-west Greater London, in a big Victorian house in Northwood with my Mum, Dad and big sister. My grandparents lived upstairs. It was always a busy, happy home. It was a great house with a lovely garden; an acre of land on which my grandfather and dad grew fruit and vegetables to their hearts' content. It sounds strange, given we were in the city suburbs, but we lived off the land. We had greenhouses full of tomatoes, cucumbers, even grapes, nectarines and beautiful succulent peaches. Fair play, I'd say, in the 1970s.

Sadly, the grown-ups in my family also had a love of flowers. I didn't. And I have recollections of utter boredom on countless Saturdays at horticultural shows. It was always the fruit and veg I loved (anything you can eat has always interested me!), so you'd always find me in my grandmother's kitchen watching her deal with the annual abundance of soft fruit from the garden.

She would transform the fruit into small pots of fresh jam after making a bubbling cauldron of sweet stickiness that wafted a fruity perfume throughout the house. To this day, whenever we cook jam at home the smell takes me back 40 years in an instant.

Both my sister, Lis, and I spent a lot of time with our grandparents. We'd perch at their dining table, tasting pot roasts, stews, cakes and stewed fruit. As a child I took all of this for granted but I now know these experiences directed and shaped my love and passion for real food and, more importantly, subconsciously formed my conviction that involving children in the great art of cooking at an early age is fundamental in pulling families together.

In our fast changing technological world it's difficult to get a work life balance right, but I believe it is of paramount importance that we still keep cooking at home. I once caught our two girls lounging in bed together on a Saturday morning, conversing and chatting through their laptops rather than talking to each other – that's scary! Let's not get mugged by technology. We need to share experiences to reinforce family bonds and friendship – get hold of some flour, sugar, butter and pastry cutters and bake together: and have fun!

Food in the UK has changed so much over the 30-odd years I have been a professional chef. During my career I've cooked both in the UK and abroad in leading international hotels, fine dining restaurants and private corporate dining rooms, for all kinds of people. For high powered businessmen, the Royal Family, the Lord Mayor of London, visiting heads of state. Amazing experiences, one and all. Who'd have thought a lippy little kid from Northwood would have ended up doing that?

When I left school as a teenager in the 1980s, I was firmly directed into catering because in those days if you weren't academically minded, careers officers shoved you towards the hospitality business. Now, in 2011, chefs have celebrity status! I've even got to go to university, kind of, thanks to an honorary fellowship from University of West London. I have to pinch myself sometimes to remember the long hours and discipline of the 1980s kitchens. I wouldn't have changed anything (well not much), but for a boy who left school with no great exam results, it's amazing having a few posh letters to add after the old name.

I am also extremely proud to be a member of the Academy of Culinary Arts (AoC), an association of leading chefs and restaurateurs who are at the top of their game. It does an amazing job in raising awareness of food, both in and beyond my industry and, very importantly, educating and inspiring young people about what they eat. As part of their AoC membership, chefs are asked to link up with local schools under the Chefs Adopt a School national charity and collectively we reach over 21,000 children every year in schools across the country.

Under this scheme, we pop into schools and teach kids not only how to cook but also how to understand and explore their taste and sensory powers. And that's how I first hooked up with the Children's Hospital School at Great Ormond Street and met the wonderful Carole Flynn, who has taught there for some 26 years.

The school was founded in 1951 with just one teacher and now has a team that teaches children and young people undergoing treatment in two London hospitals – Great Ormond Street and University College Hospital. The school aims to provide an enriching and enjoyable experience for its pupils – all ages and nationalities – and ensure some kind of normality through education for them, while also staving off anxieties that may sometimes arise among its young patients about keeping up with their studies. It's an uplifting place and I've had a truly rewarding experience teaching the kids there to cook.

I've got to say a few more words about Carole. She's a caring and wonderful person who has touched the lives of many parents and children at the school, offering them support, stability and normality when they need it most. Since working at the school, Carole, fellow Lexington director Julia Edmonds and I have been involved in putting on charity dinners and producing a cooking calendar (a major inspiration for this book) to raise money for the Great Ormond Street Hospital and its school.

I can't imagine not working with the Children's Hospital School. I get as much out of the experience as the kids. It's difficult to explain, but a letter from the mother of one of the kids, written after one of our cooking sessions, has nailed it for me. She wrote:

'My son has been very ill with colitis of the stomach and has lost all interest and love in the eating of food. In 45 minutes you managed to inspire and excite him and he is enthusiastic about cooking and eating again. I just wanted to say a huge thank you for making a difference.'

That still makes the hairs on the back of my neck stand up.
The power of food!

Enjoy the recipes in the book, cook, have successes and even some failures, it doesn't matter. Mums, dads, grandparents and kids – just get in the kitchen and have fun together.

SNACK ATTACK

THIS CHAPTER IS DEVOTED TO THE
WEEKEND, WHEN ALL THE FAMILY ARE
TOGETHER. IN MY HOUSEHOLD,
WEEKENDS ARE ALWAYS MAD, NOISY, FUN
AND TESTING! A PLATEFUL OF SNACK
ATTACKS IN TANDEM WITH A SATURDAY
NIGHT FAMILY FILM OR SUNDAY
MATINEE...PERFECT.

BIG CHEESY TWISTS

My chefs make these at work and we serve them with pre-dinner drinks. They're very moreish and much healthier than shop-bought crisps.

MAKES 20 STICKS

250g packet of good-quality ready-made puff pastry
1 tablespoon tomato purée
30g Parmesan cheese, finely grated

Preheat the oven to 180°C/gas mark 4. Then, take the puff pastry and roll it out on a floured work surface until it measures 25cm long x 20cm wide and is 5mm thick. Take a sharp knife and cut the pastry into 1cm wide strips.

Spread the tomato purée onto the pastry strips and then sprinkle them with the Parmesan cheese. Finally, make a spiral of each strip by getting hold of their ends and twisting the pastry.

Line a baking tray with silicon or greaseproof paper and place the pastry spirals onto this. (Make sure you press down each end of the pastry spirals to stop them unravelling when cooking.) Bake them for 10 minutes in the oven, until they are golden brown.

Remove them from the oven and place them onto a cooling rack, adding a little more Parmesan before they cool. Serve the twists while they are still warm in a tall glass lined with silicon paper.

TOP TIPS
These are great for grown-up drinks parties. Also, try making sweet coconut twists instead of cheesy ones: swap the tomato for honey and the Parmesan for desiccated coconut – they're great dipped in melted chocolate.

BUTTERMILK BREADED CHICKEN BUCKET

New York diners serve the best fried chicken in the world and this is my tribute to them. The secret ingredient is buttermilk which flavours and tenderises the chicken.

SERVES 4

For the marinade
285ml cultured buttermilk
2 cloves of garlic, finely chopped
1 small onion, finely chopped
2 teaspoons clear honey
1/2 teaspoon cracked black pepper
1/2 teaspoon sea salt

4 chicken breasts, cut into strips
2 eggs
75g plain flour
200g fresh breadcrumbs
75ml sunflower oil
Salt and pepper

Mix all the ingredients for the marinade in a bowl. Add in the chicken strips, making sure they are well covered by the marinade. Cover the bowl with cling film and refrigerate it overnight. The next day, drain any excess marinade off the chicken into a bowl and pat the meat dry with some kitchen paper.

In a bowl, whisk the excess marinade and the eggs together. Now, put the flour and breadcrumbs in two separate bowls/plates. You should now have three bowls in front of you. Dip the chicken strips into the flour, then into the buttermilk and egg marinade and finally into the breadcrumbs. Do this twice – you'll end up with a really crispy coating when you fry the chicken.

Put the sunflower oil in a shallow frying pan and heat it over a medium heat. When it is hot enough, drop the chicken in and fry it until the breadcrumbs turn a golden brown. You can test whether it is ready for frying by dropping a bit of breadcrumb into the oil: if it sizzles straightaway, the oil is hot enough. Don't overload the frying pan with too many chicken strips in one go, fry them in relays.

Once they are cooked, remove the chicken strips from the pan and place them onto a baking tray lined with some kitchen paper, to absorb any excess oil. Season them with some salt and pepper before serving.

TOP TIPS
Serve the chicken in something funky like a flower pot, or even an empty baked bean tin lined with silicon paper. For a whole new spin try lacing the breadcrumbs with some desiccated coconut and serve the strips with a sweet chilli dipping sauce.

STICKY HONEY AND SESAME SAUSAGES

Sausages are for life not just for breakfast! – these are proper, bona fide cocktail sausages with a twist.

SERVES 6–8

500g good quality mini
   sausages
2 tablespoons clear honey
1 teaspoon sesame seeds,
   toasted

Preheat the oven to 180°C/gas mark 4. If the sausages are joined together in a string, snip them apart with a pair of scissors, then place the individual sausages on a baking tray lined with silicon or greaseproof paper. Cook them in the oven for 10–15 minutes until they are golden brown, turning them to ensure an even colour.

Remove the sausages from the oven and while they are still hot and on the tray, add the honey and sesame seeds, making sure you coat the sausages thoroughly. Now place them in a colander to drain off any excess fat and once they have cooled slightly, but are still warm, serve them to the hordes.

TOP TIP
For a little more bite, try adding a tablespoon of wholegrain mustard at the same time as the honey.

CHELSEA PIZZA BUNS

Think of this as the posh British cousin to the Italian calzone pizza. It's a great recipe for learning how to make basic bread dough.

SERVES 8

For the pizza dough
30g fresh yeast (or 3 teaspoons dried yeast)
260ml warm water
500g strong white flour, sieved
1 teaspoon sugar
Small pinch of salt

For the filling
2 tablespoons tomato purée
50g Parmesan cheese, grated
100g mozzarella cheese, grated
100g sun-blushed tomatoes
10 basil leaves, torn

Preheat the oven to 180°C/gas mark 4. Dissolve the yeast in the warm water. Put the flour into a large mixing bowl, then add in the sugar, salt, warm water/yeast mixture and combine together with your hands until a dough forms which feels smooth and comes away from the sides of the bowl.

On a floured work surface, knead the dough for ten minutes until it is nice and elastic. Place it back into the bowl, cover the bowl with cling film and leave it in a warm place to rise until it has doubled in size. This is known as proving the dough. If you are using dried yeast, combine it with the flour before adding the warm water.

When the dough has risen, lightly flour your work surface again, remove the dough from the bowl and re-knead it briefly, re-shaping it into a ball. Next, roll the dough out into a rectangle, about 60cm long x 30cm wide.

Spread the tomato purée evenly over the dough, then scatter the grated Parmesan, mozzarella, sun-blushed tomatoes and basil leaves on top. Roll the dough up into a sausage, so that you end up with something that resembles a Swiss roll. Then cut the roll into 5cm wide slices, place these into a greased, round, cake tin or pastry ring (25cm across x 5cm deep) and leave them in a warm place (e.g. near a warm oven) to re-prove for about 30 minutes, until the slices have doubled in size.

Once the slices have risen, bake them in the oven for 25 minutes, or until golden brown. Allow them to cool slightly before tearing them apart and serving.

TOP TIP
Try substituting baked beans and cheese for the normal filling. Trust me, it's fab!

EASIEST AND TASTIEST CHEESE AND HAM TOASTIES EVER!

These simple, no-faff bites are really just a cheese and ham sandwich, buttered inside and out before being crisped up. Scrummy for brunch as well as nibbles.

SERVES 4

100g unsalted butter, melted
8 slices of white bread
8 slices of Gruyère or emmanthal cheese
4 slices of good-quality ham, thickly cut

Preheat the oven to 180°C/gas mark 4. Evenly brush the melted butter on both sides of the bread slices, making sure you go right to the edges. Then place four of the slices on a baking tray lined with silicon or greaseproof paper. On each slice of bread layer one slice of cheese, one slice of ham and another slice of cheese, then finish off with a second slice of buttered bread on top.

Cook the sandwiches in the oven for 8 minutes until the undersides are golden brown, then flip them over and cook them for a further 8 minutes so that both sides are toasted. Remove the toasties from the oven, cut them into squares and serve.

TOP TIP
Give these toasties the VIP treatment, by using Parma ham, mozzarella cheese, tomato and basil instead of Gruyère cheese and ordinary ham.

SMOKEY PAPRIKA SWEET POTATO WEDGES

I was introduced to fragrant, smoked paprika many years ago and I couldn't live without it now. It's my desert island spice. Perfect with sweet potatoes. Who needs chips?!

SERVES 4

2 large orange-fleshed sweet
   potatoes
6 tablespoons vegetable oil
1 teaspoon smoked paprika
25g Parmesan cheese, finely
   grated
1 teaspoon rock salt

For the dipping sauce
200ml crème fraîche
Small bunch of mint, finely
   chopped

Preheat the oven to 180°C/gas mark 4. Line a baking tray with silicon or greaseproof paper. Cut the sweet potatoes into wedges, rub the wedges in the oil and paprika and roast them on the tray in the oven for 30 minutes – turning them over after 15 minutes – until they are golden brown and crispy on the outside, soft and fluffy on the inside.

Meanwhile, mix the crème fraîche and mint together in a bowl. Keep this chilled until you are ready to serve the wedges.

When the wedges are done, remove them from the oven, place them on some sheets of kitchen paper and while they are still hot sprinkle the grated Parmesan and rock salt over them. Serve them quickly before they get cold.

TOP TIP
Try dusting the wedges in flour, combined with the paprika, before coating them in oil and frying them. This will give them a bit of extra crispiness.

SWEETCORN FRITTERS

All kids love fritters and these scrummy, small pancakes are bursting with flavour. They are brilliant with the buttermilk chicken (page 19) Proper soul food.

MAKES 30 SMALL
FRITTERS
.

For the batter
245g tinned sweetcorn
1 egg
100g plain flour
½ teaspoon baking powder
½ teaspoon rock salt
50ml milk

80g tinned sweetcorn
Small bunch of spring onions, chopped
1 tablespoon vegetable oil
250ml crème fraîche
Sweet chilli dipping sauce

Place all the batter ingredients into a food processor and blitz them until you have a smooth liquid.

Transfer the batter to a bowl and fold in the extra 80g of sweetcorn and the spring onions. Pour the crème fraîche and the sweet chilli dipping sauce into two separate bowls ready for serving.

Put the oil into a frying pan and heat over a high heat for a few minutes until it is just about smoking. When the oil is ready, spoon some batter into the pan using a teaspoon: enough to make baby fritters (about the size of a 50 pence piece). Cook them until they are nicely coloured on both sides (about 1 minute each side) then take them out and put them on some kitchen paper. Repeat the process until all the batter is used up, serving the fritters accompanied by the crème fraîche and sweet chilli sauce. Cool the fritters before serving them.

TOP TIP
Grown-ups should try making some elegant little dinner party starters by topping the fritters with fresh white crabmeat and dill mayonnaise.

SCRUMMY YUMMY MAINS

I BELIEVE THE BEST MAIN DISHES ARE GLORIOUSLY SIMPLE, WITH OODLES OF COMFORT FACTOR. THESE ONES HAVE SOMETHING FOR ALL THE FAMILY, BIG OR SMALL. THERE'S JUST ONE WORD FOR THEM: RESPECT!

BANGIN' SAUSAGE 'N' TOAD

'Waiter there's a frog on my plate.' 'No sir, it's a toad-in-the-hole!' Bangers in batter, with onion gravy – it's never moved out of my top 10 comfort food charts.

SERVES 4

8 good quality Cumberland sausages
4 sprigs of thyme

For the batter
170g strong plain flour
3 eggs
300ml milk
Salt

For the onion gravy
2 teaspoons vegetable oil
2 onions, sliced
2 cloves of garlic, finely chopped
Sprig of thyme
250ml beef stock
1 tablespoon gravy granules
Salt and pepper

Preheat the oven to 180°C/gas mark 4. Place 2 sausages each into 4 small ovenproof dishes – or all 8 sausages into one large ovenproof dish if you don't have 4 individual ones. Pick the thyme leaves off their stalks and scatter them over the sausages and then cook the sausages in the oven for 10 minutes.

While the sausages are cooking, make the batter. Mix the flour and eggs together thoroughly in a large bowl. Slowly whisk in the milk until you get a thick, smooth batter, then add a pinch of salt to season it. If you're in a hurry, you can blitz the batter ingredients together in a food blender.

When the sausages are ready, take them out of the oven and pour the batter around them in the dishes/dish. Replace the dishes/dish in the oven and cook the batter and sausages for a further 15–20 minutes. Don't be tempted to open the door to check on the batter's progress – you'll stop it billowing up into light, scrumptious airiness.

While the toad-in-the-hole is cooking, make your onion gravy. Heat the oil in a sauté pan over a low-to-medium heat and once it is hot enough for frying add in the onions and garlic and slowly cook until the onions begin to caramelise. Add a sprig of thyme and the beef stock and bring to a simmer for 20 minutes before adding the gravy granules. Once the granules have been absorbed and the gravy has thickened, season it with a pinch of salt and pepper.

Serve the toad-in-the-hole in the dishes/dish with a jug of warm onion gravy on the side.

TOP TIPS
Make sure your you add the batter to the sausages immediately after you take them out of the oven, when they are sizzling, as the heat will quickly seal the batter (stopping it sticking) and help it to rise. Try making mini toad-in-the-holes for drinks parties by using cocktail sausages and mini muffin moulds.

NEW YORK SLIDERS

Burgers are every child's delight. Don't buy them – they're simple to make, absolutely delicious and you control the quality of the ingredients that go into them.

SERVES 4
(3 BURGERS EACH)

300g good quality lean minced beef
½ onion, finely diced
1 egg
60g mature Cheddar cheese, grated
12 mini seeded burger buns, cut in half
4 iceberg lettuce leaves, torn
6 cherry tomatoes, sliced
Salt and pepper

In a large bowl, combine the mince, onion and egg with a pinch of salt and pepper for seasoning. Once the mixture has come together, divide and roll it into 12 little balls (about the size of a golf ball), then flatten each ball into a burger shape.

Under a high heat, grill the burgers for 5 minutes, until they are cooked through and any fat that comes off them is clear. Don't forget to flip them over while they are grilling, to colour both sides evenly. Once the burgers are cooked through, remove them, briefly, from the grill and carefully sprinkle each burger with cheese before replacing them under the grill until the cheese melts. While the cheese is melting, toast the buns so that they are ready and waiting for the burgers.

Once the cheese has melted, remove the burgers from the grill and pop them into the buns, adding lettuce and tomato to your own taste. Spear them with a wooden skewer and serve.

TOP TIPS
If beef's not your thing, these are equally delicious made with minced chicken or lamb. And don't forget to serve them with relishes or tomato ketchup.

LAMB BALLS WITH TOMATO AND DILL SPAGHETTI

A fresh dill and creamy tomato sauce, with shavings of fresh Parmesan on top of the meatballs. Fantastico!

SERVES 4
(4 MEATBALLS EACH)

500g good quality minced lamb
50g fresh breadcrumbs
1 egg
Small bunch of basil, chopped
300g spaghetti
2 teaspoons extra-virgin olive oil
100g Parmesan cheese shavings
Salt and pepper

For the sauce
2 teaspoons olive oil
1 onion, chopped
1 clove of garlic, crushed
1 teaspoon smoked paprika
2 tins of chopped tomatoes
Small bunch of dill, chopped
1 tablespoon crème fraîche

Preheat the oven to 180°C/gas mark 4. In a large bowl, combine the mince, breadcrumbs, egg and basil, together with a pinch of salt and pepper for seasoning. Once the mixture has come together, divide and roll it up into small balls (about the size of a golf ball), placing them on a baking tray lined with greaseproof paper. Then, put the meatballs into the oven and cook them for 15–20 minutes.

When the meat balls are nearly done, bring a large saucepan of water to the boil over a high heat, drop in the spaghetti and cook it out until it is soft, but still retains a firmness when you bite it.

Meanwhile, make the sauce. Heat a glug of olive oil in a saucepan over a medium heat and when sufficiently hot add in the onion, garlic and paprika and fry for about 3 minutes until the onion is soft. Now add the tinned tomatoes and cook the mixture out for a further 10 minutes. Finish the sauce off by adding and stirring in the chopped dill and crème fraîche.

Drain the spaghetti in a colander and drizzle it with the 2 teaspoons of extra-virgin olive oil to stop it sticking together. Remove the meatballs from the oven and drop them into the tomato sauce. Serve everything in a big, white bowl – drop the spaghetti in the bottom, then ladle the meatballs and sauce over the top and finish everything off with some Parmesan shavings.

TOP TIP
Try the lamb balls on their own – in a fajita or tortilla wrap, or in pitta bread – with hummus or coleslaw. Great for a lunchtime treat.

SLOW-ROASTED TOMATO AND GARLIC ON CHEESY TOAST

Every year we grow far too many tomatoes in the garden. We slowly stew, then bottle the extra ones – or make them into this lovely, moreish bite.

SERVES 4

For the cheese sauce
50g butter
50g flour
300ml milk
200g mature farmhouse
    Cheddar cheese, grated
½ teaspoon English mustard
1 teaspoon Worcestershire
    sauce
1 egg yolk

250g on-the-vine cherry
    tomatoes, halved
6 large basil leaves, torn
2 cloves of garlic, finely
    chopped
2 teaspoons olive oil
1 tablespoon tomato ketchup
½ loaf of white farmhouse
    bread, sliced
Marmite
Splash of extra-virgin olive oil

Preheat oven to 160°C/gas mark 3. Melt the butter in a saucepan over a medium heat, add the flour and cook it out to form a paste. Slowly add and beat in the milk, making sure you form a smooth sauce as you do so. Once all the milk has been added, cook the sauce for a further 10 minutes.

Take the sauce off the heat, and fold in the grated cheese, mustard and Worcestershire sauce, then quickly beat in the egg yolk. Allow the sauce to cool at room temperature. It will continue to thicken as it cools.

Place the tomatoes, basil and chopped garlic in a small roasting tray, together with a glug of olive oil. Gently fold in the tomato ketchup, then pop them into the oven and roast the tomatoes for 15 minutes until they are soft and the skin is just beginning to split.

Meanwhile, toast the slices of bread until golden brown, then spread them with some Marmite and a thick layer of the cheese sauce. Place in a warm oven for a further 10–15 minutes or until the cheese sauce turns a golden brown and caramelises. Remove the bread and cheese slices from the oven, pile on some of the tomatoes, basil and garlic and drizzle with some extra-virgin olive oil.

TOP TIP
This wonderful gooey, silky cheese sauce lasts for a couple of weeks if you keep it in the fridge, so it's perfect for kids coming in from an after school club, better still for grown-ups looking for a carb-heaven fix at the end of a party night out.

BUBBLE-AND-SQUEAK, CRISPY BACON AND A HEN'S EGG

I grew up with this Monday night special made from Sunday roast leftovers. But you don't have to have leftovers to enjoy it. I defy anyone not to want more.

SERVES 4

For the mash
4 large floury potatoes (eg maris piper), chopped
50g butter
50ml milk
Salt and pepper

For the bubble and squeak
1 onion, sliced
½ Savoy cabbage, shredded
2 teaspoons olive oil
1 teaspoon vegetable oil
8 rashers of good quality streaky bacon
4 eggs

Boil the potatoes in a saucepan of water over a medium heat until they are soft, then drain and mash them with the butter and milk until they are smooth and creamy. Add a pinch of salt and pepper to season the mash.

To make the bubble and squeak, fry the onions and shredded cabbage in a little olive oil over a medium-high heat. Once the onions and cabbage are soft, add and mix in the mash and continue to fry the mixture until the potato is golden and beginning to crisp.

Preheat oven to 160°C/gas mark 3. Line a baking tray with silicon or greaseproof paper and place the bacon rashers on top of this, covering the rashers with another sheet of silicon or greaseproof paper. Place a second baking tray on top of the paper, this will stop the bacon from curling and help to give it an extra crispy finish when you cook it. Cook the bacon in the oven for 20 minutes until it is crisp and then take it out and allow it to cool down to room temperature.

In another frying pan, gently heat the vegetable oil over a medium heat and once it is hot enough fry the eggs in this. When the eggs are cooked, dollop the bubble and squeak mixture in 4 individual serving dishes, stick in 2 rashers of crispy bacon per person and top each portion with a fried egg.

TOP TIPS
If you want to get a restaurant look, serve up the bubble and squeak in individual frying pans. And don't be afraid to add in leftover stuffing from the Sunday roast if you have it in the fridge. Anything goes!

ALL-IN-ONE CHICKEN-AND-EVERYTHING PIE

This is my lovely wife Amber's recipe. She wooed me up the aisle with this king of comfort dishes. It's irresistible.

SERVES 4

250g good-quality ready-made puff pastry

For the everything mix
300g chicken breasts, cubed
400ml fresh chicken stock
40g unsalted butter
40g plain flour, sieved
400ml double cream
2 teaspoons olive oil
1 small onion, sliced
2 cloves of garlic, chopped
100g button mushrooms, sliced
100g tinned sweetcorn
1 large head of broccoli, cooked
2 egg yolks, beaten (for glazing)
Salt and pepper

Preheat the oven to 180°C/gas mark 4. Flour a work surface and roll out the pastry on this until it is about 3mm thick. Line 4 individual pie dishes with pastry (ramekins or muffin tins work just as well if you haven't got small pie dishes) and cut 4 pastry lids to top the pies, using a round cutter slightly larger than the tins. Place the dishes and pastry tops in the fridge to chill for 30 minutes while you make the filling.

Place the chicken and chicken stock into a saucepan over a medium heat and bring to a gentle simmer for 10 minutes. Once the chicken is cooked, remove it with a slotted spoon into a bowl and leave the stock on the heat, on a rolling boil.

In another saucepan, melt the butter gently over a low-medium heat, stir in the flour so that it forms a smooth paste, then whisk this into the boiling stock to thicken it. Turn the heat down, so that the sauce is gently simmering and add in the double cream, stirring continuously as the sauce simmers for a further 5 minutes. Then, take the saucepan off the heat and allow it to cool at room temperature.

To make the filling, heat a glug of olive oil in another saucepan. When the oil is hot enough, add in the onion, garlic and mushrooms and fry them until they are soft. Add in the sweetcorn and broccoli, season the vegetables with a pinch of salt and pepper and remove them from the heat. Add the vegetables and the poached chicken to your sauce.

Remove the pie dishes and their pastry lids from the fridge and spoon in the chicken filling. Brush the underside of each pastry lid with the beaten egg yolk and place them on top of the pies, crimping the edges to seal the pies properly. Now brush the top of the lids with some beaten egg yolk. Prick a small hole in the centre of each pie, place them on a baking tray and bake them in the oven for 20–25 minutes until the pastry is golden brown. Take it out of the oven and tuck in.

TOP TIP
Try substituting the pastry lids with a Parmesan crumble for an extra layer of taste and a bit more crunch.

EASY THAI SALMON FISHCAKES WITH ASIAN NOODLES

Use any fish for this winner. I've used farmed salmon as it's a great source of omega3 (a general all-round health-tastic essential) and a sustainable fish.

SERVES 6–8

360g organic salmon, skinned and finely chopped
1 teaspoon chopped mild red chilli pepper
Small bunch of coriander, chopped
30g fresh ginger, grated
1 teaspoon garlic purée
4 tablespoons cornflour
1 lime, juiced and zested
1 egg
2 teaspoons vegetable oil
Salt and pepper

For the Asian noodles
125g egg noodles
2 teaspoons sesame oil
Small bunch of spring onions, chopped
Small bunch of coriander, chopped
1 lime, juiced and zested
Salt and pepper
Soy sauce

Put the salmon into a large bowl and then add the chilli, coriander, ginger, garlic purée and cornflower and gently mix everything together. Add the lime juice and zest, then the egg and combine these thoroughly with the fish and spice mixture. You should end up with a relatively wet and spoonable mixture. Add a little salt and pepper to season it, if necessary.

Heat the vegetable oil in a frying pan over a medium-high heat. Once the oil has reached a frying temperature, start to spoon in dollops of the fishcake mixture. You can make these as little or large as you like.

Meanwhile, blanch the noodles in a large saucepan filled with boiling water, draining them in a colander once they are soft. Heat the sesame oil in a wok or large frying pan over a high heat and when the oil is just beginning to smoke pop in the noodles, spring onions, coriander and fresh lime juice and zest and stir-fry everything together, seasoning with salt and pepper if necessary.

Tip the noodles onto a large serving plate and pop the fishcakes on top. Serve with soy sauce – and a smile!

TOP TIP
For a bit of bona fide Asian style, serve in bento boxes if you have them.

HEALTH
FOOD STORE

HERE ARE A FEW HEALTHY LIP-
SMACKERS WE CAN ALL ENJOY, WITHOUT
EVEN REALISING WE'RE ON A MINI
HEALTH KICK. I LIKE TO THINK OF THEM
AS MY HIDDEN ENERGY AND LIFESTYLE
GEMS...

STICKY SALMON AND JEWELLED QUINOA

Get the kids on to quinoa and pomegranate early: they're both super healthy, loaded with good minerals and vitamins. And salmon's not bad for you either…

SERVES 4

4 salmon fillets (125g each)
1 teaspoon olive oil
4 tablespoons good quality
   clear honey
Salt and pepper

For the quinoa
700ml vegetable stock
200g quinoa
1 pomegranate
1 tablespoon olive oil
100g Greek feta cheese, cubed
7 large leaves of basil, chopped
7 leaves of large flat leaf
   parsley, chopped
½ lemon, juiced
Salt and pepper

Preheat the grill. Brush each fillet of salmon with olive oil and half of the honey. Season them with salt and pepper, then place the fillets under a hot grill for about 10 minutes, turning them over after 5 minutes to ensure they are cooked evenly. Be careful not to overcook the fish.

Once the fish is cooked, remove the fillets from the grill, brush them with the remaining honey and leave them to cool.

Meanwhile, put the stock into a large saucepan and add in the quinoa. Bring the mixture to the boil over a medium-high heat. Once boiling point is reached, turn down the heat and simmer the quinoa for 10–15 minutes until most of the stock has been absorbed and the grain is soft and has started to split. Remove the quinoa from the heat, drain it through a sieve and allow it to cool.

While it is cooling, de-seed the pomegranate. Cut the fruit in half, place it over a bowl and carefully tap the back of the pomegranate with a heavy spoon: the seeds will just fall out.

Once the quinoa has cooled, transfer it to a large bowl and add in the olive oil, pomegranate seeds, feta, herbs and lemon juice to make a salad. Season the salad with salt and pepper, then transfer it to a serving bowl. Place the fillets on top of the quinoa salad or thread a wooden skewer through them and bring to the table on a separate plate.

TOP TIPS
For a bit of extra texture and taste, sprinkle 2 teaspoons of toasted sesame seeds over the salmon fillets when you brush them with honey after they have been grilled. And although this salad is good to go with any fish or meat, it is fab with a barbecued leg of Moroccan lamb, warm flatbreads and hummus.

SUPER FIT FLAPJACKS

These are a great way of sneaking in loads of healthy seeds and oats. Brilliant for a quick energy boost and a lunch-box winner.

MAKES 8 BARS

125g light muscovado sugar
90g unsalted butter
90g golden syrup (or good
   quality honey)
175g oats
25g pumpkin seeds
25g sesame seeds
25g flaked almonds
25g ground almonds
40g dried cranberries
40g raisins
25g dried apricots, chopped
   into cubes

Preheat the oven to 160°C/gas mark 3. Slowly melt the sugar, butter and golden syrup in a saucepan over a low heat. At the same time, put all the other ingredients into a large bowl and mix them together. Once the sugar and butter mixture has melted, take it off the heat and pour it over the dried ingredients, mixing everything thoroughly together until you have a lovely, gooey mess.

Line a baking tray (20cm long x 15cm wide) with silicon or greaseproof paper and then pour the flapjack mixture onto it, patting it down into an even thickness. Pop the mixture into the oven for 10–15 minutes until it turns golden brown, then remove the tray from the oven and let the mixture cool down before cutting it up into bars.

TOP TIP
Go more 'Club Tropicana' with your dried fruit and add papaya, pineapple and coconut into the mix.

CORNFLAKE, APRICOT AND CRANBERRY CRUNCHERS

These are so addictive, they don't last long in my house. From the first to the last crunch, it's non-stop munching.

MAKES 24

90g butter
100g caster sugar
3 tablespoons clear honey
150g cornflakes
50g dried cranberries
100g dried apricots, chopped

Preheat the oven to 150°C/gas mark 2. Melt the butter, sugar and honey in a saucepan over a medium heat until the mixture starts to froth. As soon as this happens, take the saucepan off the heat.

Put the cornflakes, cranberries and apricots into a large bowl, pour over the melted butter sauce and mix everything gently, but thoroughly, together.

Spoon the mixture into small muffin moulds/trays and bake them in the oven for 10 minutes until the crunchers are golden brown. (A silicon or greaseproof-lined baking tray is fine if you haven't got moulds: just spoon the mixture into little piles).

Once the crunchers are cooked, remove them from the oven, tip them out onto a cooling rack… and get crunching!

TOP TIP
Eat them with a dollop of organic plain yoghurt and a sprinkling of nuts for a brunch nibble.

FRUSHI

A great, fun way to get some lovely exotic fruit 'past go'. Healthy-wealthy, with a bit of sweet naughtiness...

MAKES 24

250g sushi rice
330ml water
60g caster sugar
120ml unsweetened coconut milk

For the topping
1 mango, skinned and sliced
2 kiwi fruit, skinned and sliced
6 strawberries. sliced
½ Charente melon, balled
2 blood oranges, peeled and sliced

Wash the rice under cold, running water 2–3 times. Put the water into a large saucepan, add the rice and bring it to the boil over a medium heat. Now, cover the saucepan with a lid and simmer the rice for about 10 minutes until all the water has been absorbed. Remove the rice from the heat and leave it to cool for 10–15 minutes: it will continue to swell and, at the same time, get sticky as its temperature drops.

Warm the sugar and coconut milk in a saucepan over a medium heat and stir the milk until all the sugar has dissolved. When this is done, add the milk to the rice and, once again, leave the rice to absorb the liquid.

Line a deep-sided baking tray (20cm long x 15cm wide x 2cm deep) with cling film, allowing the edges of the film to overlap the rim. Spread the rice evenly in the tray, packing it down, then pop it into the fridge for 2–3 hours. Once the rice has set firmly, remove it from the fridge and use the overlapping cling film to pop it out of the tray onto your work surface.

Now, using a sharp knife dipped in water, cut the rice up into 24 rectangles of equal length (4cm long x 2cm wide). Arrange the sliced fruit on top of the rice bites and serve your frushi with a dipping sauce of your choice.

TOP TIPS
Use a frushi-licious fresh fruit purée as a dipping sauce, or if you want to be wicked try a warm chocolate sauce. And, if you can, get hold of some banana leaves and wow everyone by serving the frushi on these with a bit of crushed ice.

SMOKED CHICKEN BANG BANG

Turn the family into celebs with this dish – a favourite of the rich and famous who dine at London's famous Ivy restaurant. I love it!

SERVES 4

For the sauce
200g good quality smooth
  peanut butter
5 teaspoons sweet chilli sauce
5 teaspoons sesame oil
5 teaspoons sunflower oil
125ml warm water
1 teaspoon soy sauce

For the chicken
4 smoked chicken breasts,
  cooked
2 large carrots, cut into fine
  strips
½ cucumber, cut into fine strips
4 spring onions, cut into fine
  strips
12 coriander leaves, chopped
2 teaspoons sesame seeds,
  toasted
1 teaspoon light soy sauce
½ lime

Over a low heat, gently warm the peanut butter in a bowl placed over a saucepan of boiling water. Once the butter has softened, remove the saucepan from the heat but leave the peanut butter in its bowl over the hot water. Gradually, whisk in the sweet chilli sauce, sesame and sunflower oils, warm water and, finally, the soy sauce. Once everything is thoroughly combined, remove the bowl from over the saucepan of water and leave the sauce to cool down at room temperature.

Remove the skin from the chicken breasts, then cut the chicken into strips. Put the chicken strips into a large bowl, then add the carrots, cucumber, spring onions and coriander and gently mix everything together, adding in the sesame seeds, soy sauce and a squeeze of fresh lime juice.

Put the chicken into a serving bowl, spoon the bang bang sauce over it and sprinkle some more sesame seeds over the top before you dish up.

TOP TIP
For some fab finger food, wrap some of the mixture in oriental rice paper, deep fry it and serve it with a warm satay dipping sauce.

WHAT-AWAY 5-A-DAY

A bit of Sicily in a bowl, this tasty salad is the perfect way to show kids how important carb-ilicious pasta is for a healthy diet.

SERVES 4

250g penne pasta
250g cherry tomatoes, cut in half
50g baby spinach leaves, washed
2 tablespoons pesto sauce
325g tinned sweetcorn
1 sweet green pepper, sliced
1 sweet red pepper, sliced
1/2 lemon
2 teaspoons extra-virgin olive oil

Bring a large saucepan of water to the boil, add the pasta and cook it until it is soft but has a little bit of firmness when you bite it. Once it is cooked, drain the pasta in a colander and refresh it under some cold running water.

When the pasta has cooled, pour it into a big serving bowl, add all the other ingredients and combine everything thoroughly. Finish the salad off with a generous squeeze of lemon juice and a slug of extra-virgin olive oil.

TOP TIP
Up the omega3 hit by adding some tinned tuna to the salad.

SUNSHINE LOLLIES

Lollies = British beach hols for me: along with windbreaks, donkey rides and sandcastles! These ones are unadulterated, pure fruit beauts.

MAKES 4

For the strawberry layer
100g strawberries
50ml water
25g sugar

For the mango layer
1 mango, peeled and chopped
50ml water
25g caster sugar

125ml plain yoghurt

Special equipment
Ice-lolly moulds and sticks.

Gently heat the strawberries, water and sugar in a saucepan over a medium heat for 2 minutes until the fruit is soft. Next, blitz the strawberries in a food processor or blender until you get a smooth purée. Pass the purée through a fine sieve into a bowl to remove the seeds and set to one side.

Now, repeat the process with the mangoes.

Next fill your ice-lolly moulds one-third full with the plain yoghurt and freeze the yoghurt until it is solid. Once the yoghurt is frozen, add another layer using the mango purée, so that the moulds are now two-thirds full and, once again, freeze the lollies until the purée has set. Finally, once the mango purée has set, top up the moulds with the strawberry purée and pop the lollies back into the freezer until the strawberry purée becomes solid. Keep them in the freezer until they are ready to be scoffed!

TOP TIP
You can save time by using any of your favourite ready-made smoothies instead of making your own fruit purée. Just make sure you buy the healthy ones.

SWEET EMPORIUM

WHAT'S LIFE WITHOUT A STICKY SWEET
TREAT? THE OCCASIONAL INDULGENCE
STOPS THOSE 'I'M NEVER ALLOWED…'
BARNEYS HAPPENING. A SWEET NOW-
AND-THEN STOPS A SWEET ROW-OR-TEN!
THESE ONES WILL KEEP YOU SMILING.

SNAKE PIT JELLY

A party winner: we used to make these for the café at the Natural History Museum in London and they always flew out of the door (or should that be slithered under it?).

MAKES 8 GLASSES

1 packet of Rowntree's strawberry or orange jelly
450ml water
1 packet of wriggly jelly snakes

Break up the jelly into cubes – and eat some (only one square)! Boil up the water, then add and gently stir in the jelly until the cubes have melted. Put to one side and allow the liquid to cool slightly.

Once the liquid has cooled a little, pour it into 8 clear, chunky glasses and put these in the fridge for about 30 minutes to chill – but don't set the jelly.

Once the jelly has chilled, take your jelly snakes and push a cocktail stick through each snake's head. Then, balance a cocktail stick across the top of each glass, letting the snake tails dangle in the jelly and allowing the snake heads to peep out over the glass tops. Now, put the glasses back into the fridge until the jelly is set to wibbly-wobbly perfection! Remove the cocktail sticks from the snakes' heads before serving.

TOP TIP
You can girly things up a bit by scattering red jelly lips in the glasses instead of snakes. Or just experiment with any of your favourite Haribo sweets.

CHOCOLATE MALTESER FRIDGE CAKE

Please drive carefully through this chocolate heaven…it's one of my faves. A crunchy, munchy fruit, nut 'n' choc fest.

SERVES 10

100g unsalted butter, softened
150g dark chocolate (preferably 72% cocoa solids)
150g good quality milk chocolate (preferably around 40% cocoa solids)
3 tablespoons golden syrup
250g plain digestive biscuits
50g raisins
50g dried cranberries
70g hazelnuts, chopped
88g packet of Maltesers

Melt the butter, both types of chocolate and the golden syrup together in a bowl placed over a saucepan of boiling water. Make sure that the water does not touch the bowl. (Breaking the chocolate up, roughly, helps it to melt quicker.) Once everything has melted, give the liquid a stir to blend it properly and then take it off the heat and allow the mixture to cool slightly.

Put the biscuits in a sealable plastic food bag and smash them up in this using a rolling pin (don't forget to make sure the bag is sealed properly first, though). Once the biscuits are nice and crumbly, add the raisins, cranberries, hazelnuts and Maltesers to the bag and give it a good shake to mix up the ingredients, then tip everything out into the bowl containing the chocolate.

Thoroughly mix all the ingredients. Line a rectangular cake tin (20cm long x 15cm wide) with cling film and tip everything into it, making sure you spread the mixture evenly, and place this into the fridge for around 2 hours until it has set. Once the mixture is solid, pop the cake out of the tin, using the cling film as leverage, cut it into squares and let the family loose on it!

TOP TIPS
Blitz the dried ingredients in a food processor, then fold them into some softened ice cream for an added dimension to an old standby. Chocolate or vanilla ice cream is best. And don't limit yourself to Maltesers: knock them off their Number One spot by using Mars Bars or Snickers instead.

LEMON MERINGUE '99' CONE

Soft, white, lemony magic. Take your time rustling up these babies (they won't melt) and master the skill of Italian meringue making.

MAKES 6 CONES

For the meringue
125g caster sugar
100ml water
2 large egg whites

6 ice-cream cones
300g lemon curd
8 mini chocolate Cadbury's Flakes (or 4 Flakes, cut in half)

NB for safety, from salmonella, use lion-branded eggs or pasteurised egg whites. I've also taken the sugar a stage further to 'hardball' to further ensure safety.

Special equipment
You will need a sugar thermometer and a piping bag with a star-shaped nozzle.

In a large bowl, mix together the caster sugar and water until a paste is formed, then put this into a heavy-based saucepan and bring the mixture to the boil. Gently place a sugar thermometer into the mixture and bring its temperature up to 121°C–130°C – this should take around 10 minutes. When you hit this temperature put a small drop of the sugar mixture into a glass of room-temperature water: this drop should keep its shape when you press it between your fingers. (technically, this is known as the 'hardball' stage).

If you haven't got a sugar thermometer, watch the mixture carefully as it heats. When it starts to turn a pale, golden brown quickly dip a metal spoon into the mixture. When you lift the spoon out, the mixture clinging to it should fall into long, silky strands. Once you reach this stage, take the mixture off the heat.

Whisk the egg whites until they just begin to hold a shape (i.e. semi-stiff). Continue whisking and carefully pour in the warm sugar mixture, using the side of your mixing bowl as a guide. Be very careful while

doing this as the sugar mixture is extremely hot.

Once all the sugar mixture has been incorporated, continue whisking the meringue for a further 4 minutes, until it is very thick, silky and glossy. Congratulations! You've just made Italian meringue.

Fill the bases of the ice-cream cones with lemon curd. Now, place the meringue into a piping bag with a star-shaped nozzle and pipe the meringue into the top of the cones, giving the top of each cone a curl like the ones you buy from the ice-cream van. Pop a flake in the top of each cone and enjoy.

TOP TIPS
CAUTION! Ban all babies, very small children and pets from the kitchen while you are adding the hot sugar mixture to the egg whites. And make sure the mixing bowl you whisk your egg whites in is spotlessly clean, otherwise you'll have trouble getting the egg white to form peaks. And last, but not least, I'd strongly advice you to only let the kids loose on this treat before midday – to avoid sugar-hit mayhem at bedtime!

NEW YORK PECAN POPCORN

Popcorn perfection – chewy, nutty and insanely moreish – this is inspired by the popcorn in New York's famous Bloomingdale's store. It pops into our house every Christmas!

SERVES 4

50g butter
200g caster sugar
2 teaspoons water
100g pecan nuts
1 teaspoon vegetable oil
150g popcorn kernels

Melt the butter, 150g of the caster sugar and water in a heavy-based saucepan over a medium heat and shake gently until it begins to bubble and caramelise to a golden brown. Add in the pecan nuts and mix them in, making sure they are well coated in the toffee.

Once this is done, carefully pour out the mixture onto some silicon or greaseproof paper and allow it to cool. Once it has hardened, break it up into pieces.

Heat the oil, slowly, in a saucepan over a low heat for 1 minute. Add the popcorn kernels to the oil, put the lid on the saucepan and listen for the pops! It should take about 3 minutes for the kernels to swell up and burst.

Once the popcorn is made, tip it into a bowl, sprinkle it with the remaining 50g of sugar and add the toffee pecans – then put a film on and munch!

TOP TIPS
If you want to be really wicked, pour some melted chocolate over the popcorn as well. For children's parties, hand out the popcorn in some jazzy mini paper bags.

SMASH-IT-UP MOLTEN HONEYCOMB

A shard of golden, crunchy honeycomb is the stuff of dreams...you just need to add a velvety chocolate sauce for a messy bit of dunkin' delight.

SERVES 4–6

100g caster sugar
4 tablespoons golden syrup
1½ teaspoons bicarbonate of soda

Special equipment
You will need a sugar thermometer.

First of all, line a baking tray with silicon or greaseproof paper and put this to one side for later use.

Put the sugar and syrup into a mixing bowl and combine them to make a paste. Transfer the paste to a heavy-based saucepan and slowly melt it over a low-medium heat. Gently place your sugar thermometer into the sugar mixture and continue heating it until it reaches 150°C. At this stage the sugar should be caramelising and going brittle (technically it's known as the hard crack point).

Take the sugar off the heat and quickly beat in the bicarbonate of soda, using a wooden spoon. Take great care as you mix, because the mixture rapidly froths up to create honeycomb.

Quickly pour the honeycomb liquid onto your silicon-lined baking tray and allow the mixture to set at room temperature. This should take about 20 minutes. Once the honeycomb has set, smash it up!

TOP TIPS
For the best crunch, eat the honeycomb on the day you make it. And serve it with some warm, melted chocolate or chocolate sauce to dunk the shards in.

MINI JAM DOUGHNUTS

I used to serve these fluffy, jammy balls in our fine dining restaurants. The grown-ups scoffed them, with huge smiles. You're never too old…

SERVES 4
(4 DOUGHNUTS EACH)

250g strong white flour
30g sugar
30g unsalted butter, cubed
20g fresh yeast (or 3 teaspoons dried yeast)
125ml warm water (37°C – body heat)
1 teaspoon salt
Vegetable oil, for deep-frying
1 jar of strawberry or raspberry jam, warmed and strained through a sieve

For the spiced sugar
8 tablespoons caster sugar
½ teaspoon ground cinnamon

Special equipment
You will need a syringe to pipe jam into the doughnuts.

Mix the flour, sugar and butter in a food mixer, using a dough hook. Whisk the fresh yeast into the warm water, then pour it into the flour mixture while the dough hook is still turning, add the salt and continue to combine everything until you have a smooth dough. (If you are using dried yeast, combine this with the flour, sugar and butter before you add the water to the dry ingredients). Cover the dough with a damp cloth and leave it to rise for 45 minutes at room temperature until it has doubled its size.

While the dough is rising, line a baking tray with silicon or greaseproof paper, then, when it is ready, flour your hands and knock back the dough on a floured pastry board or work surface. Divide and roll the dough into little balls, about the size of a 10 pence piece, placing them on a floured baking tray as you go along. Gently cover the balls with a damp cloth and allow them to rise for a further 30 minutes, until they have doubled their size.

Heat the oil in a deep-fat fryer until it reaches 170°C. If you haven't got a thermostat on your fryer, test the fat by dropping a little crumb of dough into it – if the fat sizzles, it will be ready for frying. Gently spoon in the doughnuts using a metal spoon and fry them for about 6–8 minutes until they are a deep golden brown, rolling them round in the oil as they fry to ensure an even colouring. Once they are done, take the doughnuts out and drain them on kitchen paper.

Make the spiced sugar by mixing the caster sugar and cinnamon together and roll the doughnuts in this while they are still warm. Take a knife or a skewer and prick a small hole in each doughnut, then fill your syringe with the warm jam and, following the channel you have made with the needle of the syringe, carefully fill the centre of each doughnut with the jam. Re-roll the doughnuts in the spiced sugar and serve.

TOP TIP
When cooking the doughnuts, warm the spoon you use for lifting them from the baking tray to the frying pan by, briefly, holding it in the oil. This stops them from sticking to the spoon and losing their shape.

OREO SALTED CARAMEL ICE-CREAM SWIRL

If Oreo's are milk's favourite cookie, then this may be Oreo's favourite pud!

SERVES 4

For the toffee sauce
120g unsalted butter
120g light muscovado sugar
100ml double cream
1 teaspoon rock salt

2 Oreo 6-biscuit snack packs, roughly broken up
500ml of good quality vanilla ice cream
100g slab of toffee, roughly broken up
85g bag of Mini Oreos, for decoration

To make the toffee sauce, melt the butter and sugar in a saucepan over a low heat. When the mixture turns golden brown, take it off the heat and very carefully whisk in the cream. Add the salt and allow the mixture to cool and then pop it into the fridge to thicken up the sauce.

When the sauce has thickened up enough, paint some toffee sauce on the inside of 4 glass tumblers with a pastry brush. Put some broken Oreos in the bottom of the glasses, then add a scoop of ice cream, followed by a spoonful of toffee sauce. Continue to layer up the ingredients until you get to the top of the glasses. Finally, decorate the top of these ice-cream sundaes with a broken bit of toffee slab and some Mini Oreos.

TOP TIP
Swap the Oreo biscuits for some smashed up meringue pieces (see page 68 for meringue recipe) and fresh strawberries for a spin on a classic Eton Mess.

BAKER'S SHOP

SO MANY CAKES AND COOKIES TO CHOOSE FROM, SO FEW PAGES! BUT THESE SEVEN HEADLINERS ARE UP THERE WITH THE BEST. IF YOU WANT AN EXTRA SPECIAL TREAT FOR SOMEONE, ANY ONE OF THESE FITS THE BILL.

SHORTBREAD STARS

Boxed up, these make great presents when pocket money funds are running low! Great fun for a family bake day, too. Go on, show someone you really care...

MAKES 12 STARS

150g plain flour, sieved
100g butter, cubed and
    softened
50g caster sugar
2 drops of vanilla extract

Special equipment
You will need a star-shaped
    pastry cutter.

Preheat the oven to 130°C/gas mark 1. Put the flour in a large mixing bowl, add in the butter and rub together until the mixture looks like fine breadcrumbs. Fold in the sugar, add the vanilla extract and work the mixture with your hands until it forms a ball. Continue kneading the biscuit dough until it is smooth and the bowl sides are clean. Wrap the dough in cling film and chill it in the fridge for 1 hour.

When the dough has firmed up, lightly flour a work surface and roll out the dough on this until it is about 1cm thick. Line a baking tray with silicon or greaseproof paper. Now, using your star-shaped pastry cutter, cut out some biscuits, pop these onto the tray and bake them in the oven for 30 minutes, until they are a very pale gold in colour. Remove the biscuits from the oven, cool them down and sprinkle them with a little caster sugar while they are still warm.

TOP TIP
Don't just stick with stars, get those funky pastry cutters out and make some shapes, man!

GOOEY CHOCOLATE BROWNIES

These are still the 'people's favourite'. I serve thousands of them every year. Sticky, cakey, chocolatey heaven. Need I say more...?

MAKES 12

330g unsalted butter
125g cocoa powder
4 large eggs
500g caster sugar
125g plain flour, sieved
150g hazelnuts – toasted, roasted and halved
1 teaspoon vanilla extract

Preheat the oven to 180°C/gas mark 4. Melt the butter in a saucepan over a medium heat. Once it is melted, take the saucepan off the heat and whisk in the cocoa powder, making sure that you beat out any lumps.

Break the eggs into a large bowl, then add and stir in the sugar, followed by the melted butter and cocoa. Beat the mixture vigorously until everything is thoroughly mixed together. Next add and gently fold in the flour, hazelnuts and vanilla extract. Line a rectangular cake tin (30cm wide x 25cm long is perfect) with silicon or greaseproof paper and pour in the cake mixture, making sure you spread it evenly across the tin. Level off the mixture with a spatula if necessary before baking it in the oven for 15–20 minutes.

It is important not to overcook brownies, so test the mixture after 15 minutes by piercing it with a skewer. When you pull it out, the skewer should have a little bit of stickiness on it. If it does, take the tin out of the oven immediately.

TOP TIP
Halfway through cooking, add some marshmallows onto the top of the brownie mixture. These will melt and give the brownies even more chew and goo.

COCONUT CHERRY MACAROON

These are vintage 1970s treats, a homage to my childhood. Don't forget to always eat around the cherry and save the best for last.

SERVES 6

110g desiccated coconut
75g caster sugar
1 egg white
6 glacé cherries

Preheat the oven to 170°C/gas mark 3. Combine the coconut and caster sugar in a large bowl. In another bowl, whisk the egg white until it doubles in size and stands in peaks. Now add the coconut and sugar mixture and gently fold this in. You should end up with a firm-textured mixture.

Line a baking tray with silicon or greaseproof paper and roll the mixture into golf ball-size portions, placing them on the tray as you do so. Flatten them slightly, then pop a cherry into the middle of each macaroon and cook them in the oven for 6–8 minutes, until they are light golden in colour. Take them out and cool the macaroons on a rack at room temperature. Mr Kipling, eat your heart out.

TOP TIPS

Use a tablespoon to scoop out the right quantity of raw macaroon mixture prior to rolling out your 'golf balls', but lightly wet your hands before you roll out any as this will stop the dough sticking to your hands.

DROP CLOUD MERINGUES

Another classic. Heavenly, chewy, meringuey clouds. Make these and you'll always have lots of friends.

MAKES 4 BIG MERINGUES

4 medium size egg whites
240g caster sugar

Preheat the oven to 140°C/gas mark 1. Whisk the egg whites in a food mixer until they stand up on their own in soft peaks. Continue whisking and slowly add half the sugar, making sure it is thoroughly incorporated into the egg whites.

Remove the bowl from the mixer and very slowly fold in the rest of the sugar by hand, using a large metal spoon. You should end up with a raw meringue that is thick and silky in texture and has a glossy sheen.

Line a baking tray with silicon or greaseproof paper and dust this with a little caster sugar. Using a large metal spoon, drop four big meringues onto the tray and cook them in the oven for 1 hour, or until you can lift them off the tray. They need to be hard and crispy on the outside and lovely and chewy in the middle. When they are done, cool the meringues slowly – and enjoy.

TOP TIPS
Cool the meringues in the oven – this prevents them from cracking. Serve the meringues with fruit; passion fruit or any summer berries, like strawberries or raspberries, are perfect.

FLOWER POT CARROT CAKE MUFFINS

An old-time fave, revamped and brought up-to-date by serving them in a flower pot. Stylish, funky and a treat to eat.

MAKES 8

2 eggs
200g light muscovado sugar
80ml sunflower oil
80ml plain yoghurt
4 drops of vanilla extract
2 teaspoons lemon juice
260g self-raising flour, sieved
2 teaspoons ground cinnamon
60g walnuts, roughly chopped
60g ground almonds
250g carrots, grated
60g sultanas
1 orange, finely zested

For the icing
50g unsalted butter
300g icing sugar
125g cream cheese
12 baby marzipan carrots

Special equipment
You will need a tray of muffin moulds.

Preheat the oven to 170°C/gas mark 3. Whisk the eggs, sugar and oil together in a large bowl. Then, add in the yoghurt, vanilla extract and lemon juice and combine the ingredients thoroughly.

Put the flour and cinnamon into another bowl, then add and fold in the egg mixture until everything is thoroughly mixed together. Finally, add the walnuts, ground almonds, carrots, sultanas and finely grated orange zest.

Fill 8 muffin moulds about two-thirds full with the cake mixture, then cook the muffins in the oven for 20–25 minutes. You can tell when they are done by poking a skewer into the centre of one – it the muffins are cooked, it will come out clean.

Remove the muffins from the oven and cool them on a wire rack while you make the icing. Do this by combining (or 'creaming') the butter, sugar and cream cheese together in a bowl. You can speed this up by using an electric hand whisk if you're short of time. Once the ingredients are thoroughly mixed together in a soft, smooth paste, put this into the fridge to firm up.

When the muffins have cooled, spread some icing over the top of each one and finish the cakes off by topping them with a baby marzipan carrot. If you want to be fancy, serve the muffins in little, white flower pots.

TOP TIP
Place a tray of water in the bottom of the oven when you bake the muffins. When the oven heat turns the water into steam, this will help to keep the muffins nice and moist.

LOVE HEART CUPCAKES

Cupcakes are bang on trend at the mo' and I think they'll always be a party pleaser. You'd queue up for one, now, wouldn't you?

MAKES 10

For the sponge
2 eggs
115g caster sugar
115g self-raising flour
115g unsalted butter, melted
3 packets of Love Hearts sweets, to decorate

For the buttercream icing
170g icing sugar
110g unsalted butter
Few drops of natural food colouring (any colour you fancy)

Special equipment
You will need some small paper cake cases.

Preheat the oven to 180°C/gas mark 4. Pop some paper cake cases into your cupcake baking tray. Whisk the eggs and sugar vigorously together until you have a light and fluffy mixture.

Combine the flour and butter together in a bowl, then gradually add the egg and sugar mixture to this, folding it in gently. You should end up with a smooth, stiff sponge cake mixture. Carefully spoon the raw cake mixture into the cupcake cases and then bake the cakes in the oven for 10–15 minutes until they are lovely and golden. Check to see if the sponge is cooked by sticking a skewer into one of them, it the skewer comes out clean the cakes are ready.

Remove the cakes from the oven and cool them in the baking tray on a wire rack before popping them (still in their cases) out of the tray.

While the cakes are cooling, make the icing. Whip the icing sugar and butter together, until you get a pale, fluffy 'cream', then add in a few drops of your chosen natural food colouring, beating the colour in evenly. Finally, pipe your buttercream icing onto your cakes and pop a Love Hearts sweet on each one.

TOP TIPS
Sprinkle some edible glitter onto the cupcakes as well for a bit of extra sparkle and double up the recipe quantity to spread a bit more 'lurve and happiness'.

BIG STYLEY SMARTIE COOKIES

Bright, vibrant and fun, these babies command the cover of this book. Respect!

MAKES 12

230g light muscovado sugar
115g caster sugar
170g butter, softened
2 drops of vanilla extract
1 egg
1 egg yolk
450g plain flour, sieved
½ teaspoon baking powder
Small pinch of salt
2½ tubes of Smarties

Preheat the oven to 180°C/gas mark. Combine the muscovado sugar, caster sugar, butter and vanilla extract in a large bowl until you have a smooth, creamy mixture. Gradually add and beat in the egg and egg yolk, making sure you mix them in thoroughly. Add and fold in the flour, baking powder, salt and 2 tubes of the Smarties, combining everything to form a dough. Do this carefully as you need to keep the smarties whole.

Once you have formed a cookie dough, roll this into a sausage (about 7cm across), place this onto some greaseproof paper and chill it in the fridge for 2 hours. Once the dough is really firm, take it out and slice it into thick rounds (about 2cm wide) using a warmed serrated knife and placing the cookies on a baking tray lined with silicon or greaseproof paper as you go along. Bake the cookies in the oven for 15 minutes. After about 10 minutes, take the cookies out and quickly press some extra Smarties into the top of them before popping them back in the oven for another 5 minutes.

Once the cookies are done, take them out of the oven and cool them on a wire tray. Then put the kettle on, get the kid's drinks sorted and enjoy a cuppa and a champion cookie (or two).

TOP TIP
To satisfy chocaholic cravings, make some chocolate cookies by replacing 80g of the flour with the same amount of cocoa powder.

SMOOTHIES AND COCKTAILS

THESE ARE MY FIVE FAVE KID-TASTIC
DRINKS INCLUDING AN ICONIC 1970s
COKE FLOAT AND A FRESH AND BRIGHT
PINK LEMONADE.

SUMMER BERRY BLAST

This could have easily featured in the Health Food Store chapter. It's a brilliant, easy way to get one of your five a day shots of fruit 'n' veg – and a firm fave in the Kirby family.

SERVES 4

100g raspberries
160g strawberries
1 ripe banana
100ml freshly pressed apple
  juice
10 ice cubes

Place everything in a food blender and blitz them thoroughly. Once you have a lovely, smooth, pink liquid, pour it into some tumblers and get drinking. Easy as that.

TOP TIP
Try pouring the smoothie into an ice-cube tray for freezing. The frozen cubes are great for quick, micro-lolly chilling down on a hot summer's day. Alternatively, you could add them as a finishing touch to more adult cocktails.

MELON TRAFFIC LIGHTS
AND ELDERFLOWER FIZZ

This is a healthy thirst quencher with oodles of fun and fizz. Great for children's parties. Green for go everyone!

SERVES 4

¼ of a watermelon
¼ of an ogen melon
¼ of a Charente melon
25ml elderflower cordial
200ml sparkling spring water

Special equipment
You will need a melon baller (sometimes known as a Parisienne scoop) and some little skewers.

Scoop all the melon into little balls, collecting the fruit in a bowl as you go along. Onto each skewer thread a ball of each melon for your fruity 'traffic lights'. Then, place each melon skewer into a small tumbler or shot glass.

Next, mix the elderflower cordial and sparkling water together in a jug, then top up the glasses with the fizz.

TOP TIP
Mums and dads can try swapping the sparkling water with something a bit stronger, like a sparkling white wine.

CLASSIC COKE FLOAT

A holiday special, this one keeps 'em wired all night! It's a nostalgic 1970s Wimpy classic: a pud and a drink all in one.

SERVES 4

1 litre Coca-Cola
4 scoops of good quality vanilla ice cream

Special equipment
Long sundae spoons

Fill four tall tumblers three-quarters full with Coca-Cola. Add a scoop of ice cream to each drink, enough to fill the glass. This will froth up when it hits the cola. Serve with a straw and a long sundae spoon.

TOP TIPS
This is just as fab with fizzy orange. But make sure you always put the ice cream in last, otherwise you get one big cloudy, frothy, mess. It still tastes good, but it's mucky!

CHOCOLATE TOBLERONE AND BANANA MILKSHAKE

I love Toblerone. It always reminds me of duty free shops and going on holiday. This shake gives you a fix of this classic confection and another childhood fave, banana, in one go.

SERVES 4

85g good white chocolate, broken into pieces
125g Toblerone, broken into pieces
500ml milk
2 bananas

Melt the white chocolate in a bowl over a saucepan of boiling water on a medium heat, making sure that the water does not touch the bowl. Once it has melted, take the chocolate off the heat and while it is still liquid take 4 milkshake glasses and, using a pastry brush, paint spots of white chocolate on the inside of the glasses – then place them in the fridge to set the chocolate.

Put the Toblerone pieces and the milk into a bowl and place it over a pan of boiling water, making sure that the water does not touch the chocolate. Once the chocolate has begun to melt, remove the bowl from the heat and give the mixture a good whisk. Once it looks like milk chocolate, place it in the fridge to chill.

Cut the bananas in half, removing any stringy bits, and blitz them in a food processor or blender, gradually adding the chocolate milk until the mixture is nice and frothy. Remove the cow spot glasses from the fridge and pour the chocolate shake into them.

TOP TIP
Try freezing the mixture in moulds to make ice lollies.

PINK LEMONADE

These are beautiful served in frosted glasses – and somehow very British sipped, in the garden, on a balmy summer's evening.

SERVES 8

8 lemons, juiced
100g caster sugar
500ml cranberry juice
500ml sparkling water

Put the lemon juice and caster sugar in a saucepan, over a medium heat, and bring it to the boil, stirring continuously. Remove the liquid from the heat and allow it to cool.

Once it has cooled, transfer the lemon syrup to a bowl, add the cranberry juice and put the bowl into the fridge. Once the liquid has chilled, remove it from the fridge, top it up with sparkling water and serve it in some frosted glasses.

TOP TIP
Try swapping the lemons for juicy Italian oranges.

INDEX

THANK YOU

This is the bit in the book where I get to thank all those very important people who have helped to turn my ideas into print. So, in no particular order:

From the outset, work colleague and friend Mike Sunley has lived the project with me. Thank you for your inspiration, time and belief in the book. Indeed, to all my colleagues at Lexington, particularly my fellow directors who smiled sweetly when they heard me say, 'did you know I'm writing a book?', even on the hundredth time of hearing! – thank you for the support and encouragement. A few extra-special thanks among the Lex boys and girls. Danny Moore, a particular pillar when we were sorting out food photography (the good, the bad and the indifferent); big man David Steel, who tirelessly tried, tested and tasted the food (blame him if you don't like something); Murray Tapiki who has helped at the Children's Hospital School and Emma Rogers, graduate trainee at Lexington, a shining young star, who helped me put together the recipes and make sense of my handwritten scraps of paper. Thank you to one and all.

I wouldn't have gone to the Children's Hospital School at Great Ormond Street without the Academy of Culinary Arts. So thank you AoC for giving me the tools, intros and inspiration to get involved with a wonderful bunch of people. The Academy is an amazing organisation which has been passionate about introducing young school kids to the joys of cooking and food for years – even when our government hasn't.

Huge thanks to Jon Croft and Absolute Press – for finding the time and finances for the book and for taking a punt on me in the first place. I knew we could work together, Jon, after that memorable meal which started at lunchtime and ended around 8 o'clock in the evening! To Absolute's 'Mr Creative' Matt Inwood, who kept the project on track – thank you. I knew you were a player when we put the front page together; it's amazing what you can do with a handful of Smarties! Thanks also to Claire Siggery for helping steer and implement the artworking.

Especial thanks to lovely Lara Holmes, our photographer. You have a true gift and without your eye and understanding of my vision it wouldn't have been translated onto paper. It was always going to be a huge challenge and balance to deliver a children's cookbook with real style and beauty and you played a massive part.

And to my editor Joanna Wood, a bona fide journalist who's written about me and my industry for years and who is also a good mate, thanks for the introduction to Jon and for unjumbling and making sense of all my words! It's been lovely to work together.

Also a huge thank you to Elizabeth of Mar and Carolyn Cavele of Food Matters for whipping up press interest in the book. And to Amanda Afiya, the editor of CatererSearch, for her encouragement and support throughout my career.

The 'thank you' journey wouldn't be complete without a BIG thank you to Carole Flynn and the staff at the Children's Hospital School at Great Ormond Street Hospital. Without them and their inspiring patients this book wouldn't exist. The school is truly an amazing place. I am honoured to have played a very small part in its work for the last 10 years. Carole you are a true friend, someone who deserves the biggest thank you of all for the job you do daily – your job makes cooking look easy!